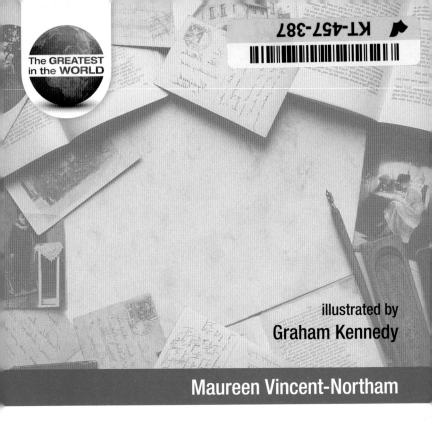

KT-457-387

illustrated by
Graham Kennedy

Maureen Vincent-Northam

The Greatest

Genealogy

Tips in the World

A 'The Greatest in the World' book

www.thegreatestintheworld.com

Illustrations:
Graham Kennedy
gkillus@aol.com

Cover & layout design:
the designcouch
www.designcouch.co.uk

Cover images:
© Alan Dunlop-Walters; © Michaela Stejskalová; © Nikolay Suslov
all courtesy of www.fotolia.com

Copy editor:
Bronwyn Robertson
www.theartsva.com

Series creator/editor:
Steve Brookes

First published in 2007 by Public Eye Publications

This edition published in 2007 by
The Greatest in the World Ltd., PO Box 3182
Stratford-upon-Avon, Warwickshire CV37 7XW

Text and illustrations copyright © 2007 – The Greatest in the World Ltd.

A CIP catalogue record for this book is available from the British Library
ISBN 978-1-905151-72-1

Printed and bound in China by 1010 Printing International Ltd.

To Ken and Elsie Kilminster,
the best parents I could have wished for.

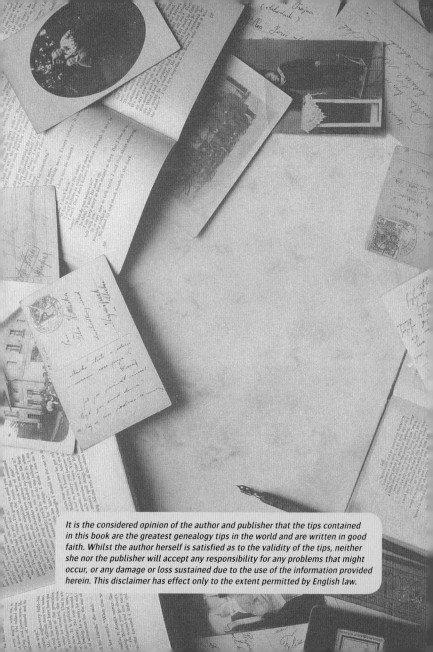

Contents

Introduction

Never before has genealogy been as popular as it is today, but what is it that makes us so inquisitive? Perhaps it's a family legend of royal connections, a secret linked to a notorious forebear, or simply a burning curiosity to know who we really are.

Whatever the reason, there are intriguing ancestors – and plenty of them – in everyone's family tree. Think of it like this: for every generation we go back, we double the number of our direct ancestors – two parents, four grandparents, eight great grandparents, and so on. By the time we reach the 16th century, we could each be looking for over one thousand people!

But for me, genealogy isn't just about drawing up a pedigree with a long list of names that go back to the year dot. It's about widening our knowledge of the times our ancestors lived through, finding out what they did, and getting to know the sort of people they were. By doing this, we bring our own unique history to life.

In my role of researcher, I've shared in people's joys and frustrations; had a great deal of fun, and met some wonderful people – and a few eccentrics – along the way! I've been asked to prove connections to several famous people in history, from monarchs to pioneers of the American Wild West! But all of my clients have had one thing in common – a fascination for discovering their personal genealogy.

Everyone's family history is different. The tips in this book will show you the best tricks of the trade; how to begin your research from scratch; what the most useful records are, and where to find them; what to do if you get stuck; and how to create your very own archive. Below I have listed the basic 'tools' you will need — in addition to the enthusiasm and enquiring mind that you already have!

You're about to set off on a remarkable quest ...

Good luck and happy hunting!

Maureen

BASIC GENEALOGY KIT:

- Notebooks
- Pencils (pens are not permitted in archive offices)
- Tape recorder
- Digital camera
- Magnifying glass
- A copy of The Greatest Genealogy Tips in the World!

"Some people are your relatives but others are your ancestors, and you choose the ones you want to have as ancestors. You create yourself out of those values."

Ralph Ellison

In the beginning

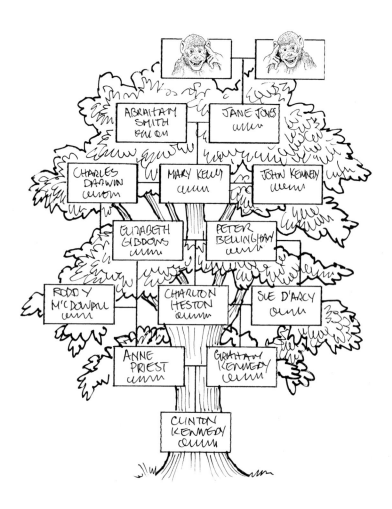

chapter 1
In the beginning

There are few things more satisfying than building your family tree – even if you do find a skeleton or two lingering in a closet! But, before you start searching further afield, gather together all the evidence you can from those nearest to you. No matter how trivial it may seem at first, just remember that small clues lead to great discoveries!

Questions, questions

One thing is certain; not everyone in your family will share your enthusiasm for uncovering the past. In fact, it's probably true to say that some won't give a toss. Never let this fact deter you. Instead, put together a questionnaire and distribute it doggedly to any relatives you think might be able to help. If you need to mail your questionnaire, it's a good idea to enclose an SAE – thus ensuring they have one less excuse not to reply! Here are my lucky seven questions.

1. Is there a family Bible, or any family papers, in your possession?
2. Do you have any old birth, marriage, or death certificates?
3. Thinking back to your childhood, what older family members do you remember?
4. How were they related to you and to each other?
5. Have you photos of any of these people?
6. Do you know exactly where they lived?
7. What were their professions?

Test the waters

Two tips in one here! If you're very new to genealogy, my first tip is to start with the branch of the family you're most familiar with. My second tip is to check out a few things you already have information about so that you can get a good feel for how the various systems and documents work. Try starting with parents' or grandparents' birth or marriage records, or look up a grandparent or great grandparent on the 1901 census.

On the spot

It will really pay off if you can get a few of those distant cousins involved in your family history project. If they still live in the same part of the country that your shared ancestors came from they will have much easier access than you do to all those lovely records at the local County Archives!

FAMILIES ARE NOT JUST FOR CHRISTMAS
Don't you just love all those family gatherings? If your response to that question was in the negative, just think of the rich store of information you can tap into at these events. My tip is to carry your notebook to every wedding anniversary party and any other assorted family knees up!

Photo opportunity …

For some unfathomable reason just about everyone seems to have the odd photo or two of a complete stranger in their collection. Who are all these people, and what are they doing in your family album? Show these snaps to any family member you think might have an inkling of who these mystery people are. They could turn out to be an important link.

Those were the days!

They say it's good to talk, and it is – especially to older relatives. A person's short-term memory might begin to fade with age but often their earliest recollections are as sharp as ever – and a gentle prod can work wonders!

- What sort of home did they live in; what about the furniture, garden and the neighbourhood?
- Get them to tell you about their childhood. Did they have a favourite toy and what games did they play?
- Find out all you can about social gatherings and important family events. Did they take holidays or observe certain religious festivals?
- Ask about their working life.
- Were they or others in their family, members of a club or society?

DID YOU KNOW …
Until the 1840s, children didn't have to attend school.

What are they wearing?!

The clothes worn in old photos can tell you quite a lot – and not just that your ancestors had no dress sense! Those casual snaps taken in 'work' clothes reveal something of a person's social status; while more formally posed ones, with them sporting the newest trendy clobber, will be better at indicating the time period.

Broaden your outlook

It's possible that some papers vital to your research weren't passed down through your direct family line and Great Aunt Flossie might have been entrusted to preserve the dynasty's all-important memorabilia, rather than your own dear Granny. Widen your search to include more distant family members.

The dating game

A word of warning if you're trying to date an old photo by studying the sitter's clothes: not everybody wore the latest fashions, whether by necessity or design, so a certain style of dress or suit might have been worn for quite a long period. For older people especially, fashion was less important and the style of dress didn't change a whole lot over the years.

> **DID YOU KNOW …**
> An Act of Parliament in 1795 levied an annual tax of one guinea on the use of hair powder.

NOT JUST A PRETTY FACE ...

Look at what's beyond the person in a photograph – the landmark, house, shop, park and so on are the things that will help you pinpoint where the picture was taken. Ask other family members to help out if you don't recognise the places yourself.

A flash of inspiration!

Formal studio photographs are often stamped with the name and address of the photographer, which can help you to date an old picture. Search in old trade directories to find when the studio was in business. The town where the studio was situated might be where your ancestor once lived, so will be worth further investigation.

A box of delights!

Rummage in that ancient biscuit tin for a few treasures!

- LETTERS
  Letters are normally dated and usually have the sender's address as well as an address on the envelope. Apart from the letter's content, you can discover something about the recipient and family relationships by noting how the letter is worded – Dear Mrs, Dearest Aunt Maude, My darling, and so on.

- POSTCARDS
  Long forgotten picture postcards could give you a useful address as well as a date (if you can make out the postmark).

- INVITATIONS
  People often keep wedding invitations and these can be very useful to find. They'll supply you with dates, the names of the happy couple and where the marriage was to take place, along with some detail of the bride's parents.

- CLIPPINGS
  Newspaper clippings are kept for all sorts of reasons, though if you come upon a cutting for Mrs Feelgood's Bear Grease Cure All, this might not be immediately relevant to your research! Make a note of any names you don't recognise. If the news item offers an important clue but the clipping isn't dated, search the newspaper archives to find the issue in which it appeared.

Dear diary

As personal documents go, they don't get much better than
an old diary or journal. They can tell you a lot about your
ancestor's personality and offer clues about what life was like
for them. If you're lucky enough to find one, look for references
to other people, dates, and locations where events took place.
But remember that diaries and journals can be biased and give
personal opinions rather than facts.

Caution – family pedigree ahead!

Should you come upon Great Uncle Walter's carefully drawn
family tree lying in a shoebox at the bottom of a trunk behind
a hat stand in the attic, try to curb your excitement until you've
begun to check its legitimacy. Unlike today, when we have so
many records easily and freely available to us, there was a time
when people quite often compiled family pedigrees using little
more than guesswork and rumour.

It wasn't too difficult to make the wrong assumptions; certain
surnames are fairly commonplace in some areas, but are rare
in others. It would have been easy enough to find that unusual
name on a headstone, or inscribed on a church plaque, and
have wrongly linked together two unconnected families.
Likewise, there might well be several families in a village –
and dozens in a town – who share a very common surname
but who are unrelated.

Old Walter's pedigree could also be incomplete, showing only
the male lineage with but a mere nod in the direction of the
female family members – time for you to get better acquainted
with the rest of your family and fill in all those blank spaces.

Those old souvenirs

If one of your ancestors has passed down a lot of holiday souvenirs from a particular place it suggests they were frequent visitors. When holidays were rarer and travelling around the country wasn't simply a question of zipping off in the 4x4, that collection of 'Greetings from Bournemouth' knick-knacks might mean they lived fairly close or had other relatives in the area.

A family Bible

Families recorded the details of births, marriages, and deaths in family Bibles long before civil registration began, which gives you a head start in the genealogy race if you find one has been passed down through your own family. Be sure to ask a wide circle of family members if such a book exists, as it could have ended up in the hands of what has since become a more distant branch of your family tree.

Sticking around

If your ancestors were landowners, farmers, or had the sort of family business that passed from father to son then I have good news for you. It should be a darn sight easier to track them down as it's likely the children won't have strayed too far from the fold (or Father's money), and you'll probably find the family living in the same parish for several generations. But while not every family stayed put in the same village or the same part of town, a great many didn't venture too far away either. If your trail goes cold in one parish, try looking first in the adjoining ones.

Lend an era!

Most libraries stock a good selection of illustrated local history books showing towns and villages, houses, businesses, and transport. Use your library card and put your ancestors' lives into context by reading a broader history of the district in the time period in which they lived. You could come across some local detail that aids your own research.

Crest fallen!

There are a lot of families who have the right to a coat of arms – though many more who don't! Be prepared to discover that the family crest embossed on Great Granny's silver teapot is in fact a fake, as the Victorians were taken in big time. Well let's face it, who could resist when faced with advertisements claiming to provide a genuine coat of arms to anyone who sent in their surname and place of origin? Check if the crest is authentic by submitting the details to the College of Arms.

Around 20 per cent
of Americans can
trace their ancestral
roots back to England,
and around 16 per
cent can trace theirs
back to Ireland.

In the beginning …
Chapter summary:

- Compile a questionnaire to distribute to family members.
- Research the branch of your family most familiar to you.
- Learn how family history documents work.
- Take along a notebook to all family occasions.
- Talk to older relatives.
- Get in touch with more distant family members.
- Look at old family photographs.
- Beware unverified family pedigrees.
- Newspaper cuttings can offer vital clues.
- Check out local history books.

We all grow up with the weight of history on us. Our ancestors dwell in the attics of our brains as they do in the spiraling chains of knowledge hidden in every cell of our bodies.

Shirley Abbott

A helping of
civil sources

chapter 2

chapter 2
A helping of civil sources

Of course, nowadays our births, marriages, and deaths are officially recorded, and these records are kept by the General Register Office (GRO), but up until July 1837 there was no official registration in England and Wales. In Scotland civil registration began in 1855 and in Ireland, in 1864. If you're looking for earlier dates, the parish registers are what you need.

The other really helpful civil resource is the census – the population survey taken by the government every ten years. This began in 1801 and, although a few earlier censuses still exist, the 1841 is the first one that's any real help, and even with this one, things could be better! The census records have a 100-year closure period but you can look up lots of useful details about your ancestors from 1841 to 1901.

> **DID YOU KNOW ...**
> By 1839, divorced mothers 'of good character' were allowed the right of custody of their children under seven for the first time, but needed the Lord Chancellor's permission.

It's all in the timing

The GRO indexes are listed alphabetically by surname, but to make things more interesting for you they've arranged those lists in quarter years: March, June, September and December. If your ancestor was born, got married or died during January, February or March then the event should have been registered in the March quarter and so on. But this doesn't always follow!

- Events that actually took place towards the end of a quarter will likely not show up until the next quarter.

- A birth, marriage, or death that took place in December of one year might not have been registered officially until the March quarter of the following year.

- Some people didn't register an event at all, especially in the years before 1875, when tougher measures were introduced!

Initial errors

The GRO indexes are lists which have been transcribed from the original registrars' returns and in some cases might have been copied incorrectly or even misheard by the registrar in the first place. If you haven't turned up a surname in the index where you think it ought to be, have a go at substituting similar looking initial letters – C for G, M for N and P for R – Norris might have become Morris or Probert might be listed under Robert for example.

Or try adding or taking away the letter H – it's possible that the registrar thought someone was 'dropping his aitches' and so wrongly 'corrected' Alford to Halford and so on.

Name dropping!

A forename chosen by the parents and registered at birth might be different from the one by which that person was later known. This doesn't mean anything sinister and is more likely to be a case of the person disliking the name or changing it to avoid confusion when the child's father had the same handle!

Quite often people swapped names around and used their middle one. If you've searched the GRO lists without luck, try using the person's other forename if this is known to you; if you don't have this information, search by surname and take note of any entries where the middle name is the one familiar to you.

Marriages: the perfect match …

In the GRO indexes, although they share the same reference number, couples' names are listed separately so you need to search both names (in the same year and quarter) and then check that the reference numbers match. To make things easier, search the least common surname first.

Hospital visiting

Women weren't always sent home from hospital a few minutes after giving birth! In the times when they were allowed to spend a week or two recovering from the ordeal of junior's arrival, it was common for a registrar to visit the hospital on a regular basis to record each child's birth. This can mean a birth showing up in the index in the district where the maternity hospital was situated, which might have been some distance from where the child's family actually lived.

More hospital drama!

Your ancestor could have died in a hospital that wasn't in the same area in which he or she lived, and so the death registration might not show up where you would expect to find it. If this happens, it's quite likely you'll find the death was registered where the hospital was located – perhaps miles from their home and possibly even in a surrounding county.

Save time and money by applying direct

Once you've found your ancestor's birth or death in the GRO indexes, it's quicker and cheaper (£7 at present) to send for a copy of the certificate from the register office where the event was originally registered, than from the General Register Office. There's a list of addresses and contact details at: **www.fhsc.org.uk/genuki/reg**.

Supply any information you know to be correct. Make the cheque payable to the Superintendent Registrar and ask that they issue the certificate only if it corresponds with the information you've supplied – that way you'll get your money returned if the details don't match! For a birth it's useful if you can tell them:

- The year and quarter in which the event is listed in the indexes.
- The child's name.
- Father's name if known.
- Mother's maiden name if known.
- The parish in which they lived.

Six really useful things about a death certificate ...

Of course it goes without saying that these notifications confirm a death but take a look at a few of your ancestor's certificates and they might help you fill in some valuable extra details – and that's always a good thing.

1. The certificate will give you the actual date of death rather than the burial date found in a parish register.

2. You'll find out the place he or she died. This might not be where you thought, but might instead give you some, yet unexplored, avenues to follow.

3. It will state the age at death, though this might not always be accurate if the informant didn't know the person well.

4. The person's rank or profession is also given, which could open up some new areas of research.

5. It'll give the cause of death. If this was an accident, such events are often recorded in a local newspaper. It could also suggest an occupational hazard or an epidemic.

6. The informant's details are listed, including name, address, and relationship to the deceased person. Registering a death was normally the task of the next of kin so it's worth checking out these names – a woman informant who has a different surname might be a married daughter or sister, for instance.

Finding a child's parents

When looking for the marriage of a child's parents, work backwards from the child's birth or baptism. But don't give up too soon – the child could be the youngest of a very large family with the marriage taking place 20 years before! If you still can't find the marriage, work forwards from the child's birth, the couple might have married after the child was born.

And by the same token …

If you have trouble locating the birth of the eldest child of the family in the GRO indexes, try searching under the mother's maiden name. But a marriage might take longer …

You'll be on a hiding to nothing if you ask a registrar for a marriage certificate when you've no idea where the wedding took place! Unless you can supply this info, you're backing a loser here as, with no parish index, the registrar might have to search the registers of every church and chapel in the district before coming upon the one you want. Much less hassle to apply direct to the GRO.

Quick tip

BRITISH BIRTHS, MARRIAGES, AND DEATHS AT SEA
Contact the National Archives if you're looking for details about an ancestor who was born, married, or died at sea or abroad between 1831 and 1958. They hold the civil registration for these events, known as (this will just roll off your tongue) the Registrar General's Miscellaneous Non-statutory Foreign Returns.

Where can you see the census records for free?

The only place that has a complete set of census returns for England, Wales, the Channel Islands, and the Isle of Man is the Family Record Centre in Islington, London. But indexed digital copies from 1851 to 1901 can be viewed at the National Archives. Both these resources are free if you visit the centres in person. The Family Search website has a free searchable database for the 1881 British census.

County Archives and local reference libraries hold copies of the censuses for their own district on microform.

Six helpful things you can glean from a census return ...

1. The name or number of the house and the street your ancestor lived in.
2. Who the head of the household was.
3. A list of all the people who were in the house and how they were related to the householder.
4. Their ages and marital status.
5. Their occupations.
6. Their places of birth.

DID YOU KNOW ...
In 1885, the legal age of consent was raised from 13 to 16.

Census or nonsense!

Each census covered the period from Sunday night to Monday morning and every household was required to fill out a form. The completed form gave details of who was in the household during this time and was collected the following day by the enumerator, who then transcribed the information into another book. Sounds simple enough you might think, but things didn't always go according to plan. Watch out for mistakes due to:

- The instructions on the forms not being fully understood.
- People not able to spell.
- The enumerator wrongly transcribing what someone had written.

Carry on searching

When using the census returns, if you track down the ancestor you've been searching for in a particular district, don't stop looking! Note any entries of the same surname in that location as they might turn out to be related, especially if it isn't a common name.

Age concerns!

It might look like it, but people weren't necessarily lying about their ages on the 1841 census. Children under the age of 15 had to have their exact age listed but anyone older had his or her age rounded down to the nearest five so you must allow for certain anomalies. For example, if a woman was 24 then she would be recorded as 20, even though she married at 16 and has an eight year old child!

But don't rule out fibbing altogether ...

From 1851, all ages were meant to be given accurately but people could have had their reasons for telling a few porkies!

- A person might have pretended they were younger if they felt their job was at risk if their employer knew the truth.
- Someone under 21 might say they were older in order to rent property.
- People were proud to reach old age so someone quite elderly might have really tried to impress by adding on a few extra years!

A little forgetfulness ...

Once you've discounted silly census rules and deliberate economies of truth, you can put down most inconsistencies in your ancestors' ages – when compared with an earlier or later census – to poor memory. People forget their own ages and the ages of their spouses and children all the time – so nothing new here! And maybe someone filling in the details on behalf of an elderly relative wouldn't have known their age.

Quick tip

CONTEMPLATING NAVAL CENSUSES
British naval and merchant vessels, both at sea and in port, were included in the census returns from 1861. These are certainly worth looking into, though unfortunately they're not complete.

chapter 2

Some final thoughts on ages

Remember that the census wasn't taken on the same date each time, so any discrepancy might be accounted for by your ancestor having celebrated a birthday during these weeks.

- 1841 – 6th June
- 1851 – 30th March
- 1861 – 7th April
- 1871 – 2nd April
- 1881 – 3rd April
- 1891 – 5th April
- 1901 – 31st March

Surname spelling slip-ups

When all the other data matches up, don't discard a census entry just because the surname isn't spelt the way you think it should be. There are several reasons why spellings differ; the census enumerator could have misread what was written on the form, or your family might once have used another spelling. And if you're using a census index, an error could have occurred during the indexing process.

Farmer forebears

If your ancestor was a farmer you'll get some added data for your family history file from the censuses that were taken between 1851 and 1881. During these dates the farm acreages were also specified on the returns and also whether someone was an employer or an employee.

Nickname nightmare!

The nickname your ancestor was known by to family and friends could have been given in the census records rather than their proper name, so you might need to do a little lateral thinking to sort them out. Here are ten popular names and their commonly-used nicknames.

1. Bella, Betsy, Lisa = Elizabeth
2. Daisy, Meg, Peggy = Margaret
3. Dodie, Dolly, Dora = Dorothy
4. Hettie = Esther
5. Jack = John
6. Jenny = Jane
7. Kate, Kitty = Katherine
8. Molly, Polly = Mary
9. Sadie, Sally = Sarah
10. Nell, Nora = Eleanor

By 1852, burials at most urban churchyards were forbidden for public health reasons, and new burial grounds, set up by local councils and private companies, were put in place.

Jumping to conclusions

Unlike the later censuses, the 1841 doesn't show the relationship of each individual to the head of the household and sometimes identifying who's who in this census will be purely guesswork on your part! A man and woman living at the same address and who share the same surname could be man and wife, but they might also be brother and sister or father and daughter.

How big was your ancestor's home?

You can fill in all sorts of riveting detail about your ancestor's life from the census forms they completed. For instance, you'll know whether their living accommodation had fewer than five rooms, as this information had to be included on the census returns from 1891.

Quick tip

A TIP FOR WHEN YOU DON'T KNOW A WOMAN'S MARRIED NAME

This can be time consuming and works best if the woman in question had a not-too-common forename or if you can consult an index for a particular area to limit the search results. Investigate any females who might be within the correct age range by searching her first name only. Once you have a list of promising ones, check where each was born to (hopefully) find a match!

Spotting an illegitimate child on the census

It isn't always possible to spot an illegitimate child but here are a few things to look out for:

- A child who retains his or her mother's maiden name.
- A child's name at the bottom of the family list and out of age sequence.
- A child who is referred to as 'wife's son or daughter'.

Someone's missing from the family group …

If a member of the family hasn't been included on the census form, but you're pretty certain they hadn't left home permanently at this time, look for them on the census entries of other close relatives, where they might have been visiting.

DID YOU KNOW …

After 1834, families in the workhouse were segregated.

Four ways to check if the place of birth is correct

From 1851, the place of birth was included on the census, but not everyone got this right, which can mean locating a baptism record gets a bit tricky! The information given by parents about their child's place of birth is usually correct, but an older person might have mistakenly given the place where they grew up rather than where they were born. Here are four top tips to help you track down your ancestor's place of birth.

1. The birth certificate will give the parents' address.
2. Look at a sibling's census entry to see the place of birth they've given.
3. If you have the parent's census details, try searching records from their parishes.
4. Check later censuses. Your ancestor might have given different information at a later date.

DID YOU KNOW …
A fire in Dublin in 1922 destroyed thousands of records, including the census returns from 1861 to 1891.

A helping of civil sources
Chapter summary:

- There is no civil record of births, marriages, or deaths before 1837.
- You might need to search the GRO indexes beyond your 'known' dates.
- Check names using a variety of different spellings.
- The informant on a death certificate could prove to be a valuable lead.
- Birth and death certificates are cheaper from the local register offices.
- Local archives and libraries hold censuses for their own district.
- From 1851, the place of birth is shown on the census returns.
- Ages on the censuses aren't always correct.
- People sometimes used nicknames on the census.
- Remember to check the workhouse census.

"The lives of great men all remind us we can make our lives sublime and departing leave behind us footprints on the sands of time."

Thoreau

Perusing the Parish records

chapter 3
Perusing the Parish records

A mongst other things, the parish records include the church registers, which are the documents you need when tracing your family tree beyond 1837. In England and Wales some parish registers date back to 1538, in Scotland to 1558 and in Ireland to 1634. Remember though that the parish registers record the dates of baptisms and burials rather than births and deaths found in the civil registration lists.

A second opinion

Some old parish registers are in a very sorry state, with damaged and discoloured pages or with entries looking for all the world like they were written using invisible ink. It's really just a matter of luck whether the registers you will need to consult were written by the vicar who prided himself on his neat columns or by the one who over-zealously filled every available space with an illegible scrawl!

Luckily, from the late 16th century, copies of the register entries were sent in annually to the diocesan registrar. These copies are called the Bishop's Transcripts and are usually held at County Archives. They're sometimes in a better condition than the parish registers, so my tip is to use these to verify information that's difficult to read in the registers.

Seeing double!

If your ancestors appear to be baptising two children with the same name within the space of a few years, don't panic, you're probably not seeing things. Quite often when a child died a new baby was given the same name. If you come across one of these repeated baptisms in your research always look in the burial register for an entry for the first child.

Family baptisms

You might not always find a baptism where you'd expect to find it. If you have difficulty locating one, search further into the register before throwing in the towel as some families had their entire brood baptised as a job lot!

Baptising illegitimate children

These baptisms are easy enough to spot as they generally record the mother's name only. But the word the clergy used to describe the child's circumstances varies quite a lot. Look for any of these:

- Illegitimate
- Spurious
- Base
- Supposed
- Baseborn
- Misbegotten
- Bastard

Is he the father or isn't he?

'Reputed' and 'imputed' are a couple of words that crop up from time to time in a baptism register. Something like: "Mary the reputed daughter of James Fletcher by Ann Jones" will tell you that James has admitted paternity. But if 'imputed' is used it means everyone's pretty certain James is the father but he's owned up to nothing!

Sometimes Dad's name is handed to you on a plate!

Occasionally, tracing the father of an illegitimate child isn't all that difficult. His name might conveniently appear in the baptism register as in, "Mary Jones, daughter of Ann Jones and James Fletcher".

A child given two surnames in the baptism register is also a clue worth following: "Mary Fletcher Jones, daughter of Ann Jones".

More info in parish registers after 1813

Some bright spark in the early 19th century came up with a pretty smart idea because, after 1813, parish registers were produced complete with pre-printed pages. This enabled more information to be included as a matter of course, so a baptism entry will give you not only the parents' names but the area in which they lived (later their full address) and the father's occupation. It's also quite common to find the child's date of birth squeezed into the later entries.

Marriage rules OK!

Certain new rules were brought in affecting marriages after 1754, which makes life a lot easier for family historians.

1. Marriages must be preceded by the calling of banns or by the issuing of a marriage licence.
2. A record should be kept in an appropriate book.
3. Entries in the book should be signed by the couple and by witnesses to the marriage.
4. The ceremony must take place in the parish where the bride or groom resided.

Did you know?

That after 1837, a photocopy of the marriage entry in the parish register is as good as having a copy of the marriage certificate – and a lot cheaper? What you'll learn is:

- The couple's full names and addresses.
- Their ages – earlier entries may just say 'of full age'.
- Their occupations.
- Their fathers' names and occupations.

Witnesses, clues and detective work

The parish register entry, or the marriage certificate, will also give you the names of two people who witnessed the marriage. As these witnesses were often related to the happy couple, they can throw up some valuable clues for further research; perhaps a married sister's new surname or the name of a brother's wife.

Quick tip

Married by banns

If you have trouble finding a marriage in the parish register try searching the banns books. The banns are a public announcement of a forthcoming marriage and are announced in church on three Sundays preceding a marriage. If the marriage doesn't take place within three months of the last announcement, the process begins all over again.

Married by licence

Copies of marriage licences can often be found in County Archives. A couple might have obtained a licence rather than have banns read out in church if they wanted to marry in a hurry, or if they didn't want the parish gossips to know their business! A marriage licence required two bondsmen to stand as guarantors and these were usually relatives.

> **DID YOU KNOW …**
> Prior to the 18th century, clergymen were known as clerics or clerks.

The ancient custom of newly weds drinking a beverage of diluted honey during their first month of marriage, led to the word 'honeymoon'.

Civil marriages

Marriages solely by licence or banns continued until 1836, after which couples could marry in a civil ceremony conducted by a registrar. If you can't locate a marriage in the parish registers, try looking up the entry in the General Register Office indexes – a copy of the actual marriage certificate will indicate where the wedding took place.

Where did they bury him?

There's always the odd ancestor who's never where you expect him to be! If you can't find his burial in the parish he died in, try the one where he was born – he might have wanted to be laid to rest near other members of his family.

National Burial Index (NBI)

The Federation of Family History Societies is in the process of collating an index of burial records. To date, the extracts contain over 13 million records taken from parish, non-conformist, and cemetery burial registers. The NBI is sold on CD-ROM but most County Archive offices and some reference libraries have copies that you can consult free of charge.

> **DID YOU KNOW ...**
> Before dedicated asylums were set up in the 19th century, the mentally ill were sent to the workhouse.

A possible indication of a non-conformist wedding

Non-conformists (or dissenters) were all those who followed a religion other than the Church of England. Between 1754 and 1837 only marriage ceremonies in the Anglican Church were legal – with Jews and Quaker marriages being the exception.

This isn't a foolproof system, but if you find a couple marrying by licence in their local church, then find no christening for the couple's children in the parish register, it could mean they were non-conformists.

A non-conformist baptism

The keepers of the non-conformist chapel books often gave more detail about those who were baptised than the parish clerk did in his registers. As well as the usual date, names, place of residence (and later, the father's occupation), the chapel books often give the mother's maiden name and the child's date of birth.

Non-conformist burial entries

As with the baptisms, the non-conformist burial register entries tend to supply some very useful extra booty! Together with the date, name of deceased, their last address and occupation, both parents' names are often listed when a child is buried and on a married woman's entry her husband's name is sometimes given.

Buried in the local churchyard

Check the parish church register, too. Not every non-conformist sect had a burial ground of its own, so members were buried in a part of the local churchyard. My tip is to look for a change in the way the clerk normally wrote up the burial entry in the parish register; he might have described the poor soul's laying to rest as 'interred' or possibly, 'hurled'!

Quick tip

LATER NON-CONFORMIST BURIALS

The burial of a non-conformist from around 1850 often took place in the unconsecrated part of a cemetery that was run by a local burial board, rather than in a churchyard.

Parish burial registers or internment registers – spot the difference!

The parish churches keep registers to record the details of funerals which take place in the church. But whether or not a funeral was conducted in church, the cemetery where a person is laid to rest also holds a register of the internments. These cemeteries are usually run by district councils.

DID YOU KNOW ...

A Victorian female servant earned about £50 a year.

"That'll be one of those non-conformist weddings then will it?"

Distant dissenters

Not all areas had their own non-conformist chapel, so if your ancestors were dissenters they might have had to trudge miles to attend the nearest meeting of their chosen sect. Be prepared to circle a wide area from where they lived to find any details about them.

Who holds the records?

Some non-conformist registers were never handed in centrally and might still be languishing somewhere within the relevant chapel. County Archives hold a number of non-Anglican registers and they should be able to advise you on the whereabouts of others.

Irregular marriages in Scotland

Church marriage registers in Scotland generally contain the proclamation of banns only. Irregular marriages (where no banns were called) could come about by a promise made in public, mutual consent, or by cohabitation with habit and repute. A list of custodians and owners of all the known existing records of Scottish irregular marriages is displayed on the General Register Office for Scotland website. **www.gro-scotland.gov.uk/famrec/hlpsrch/summrmar/ runmar.html**

Quaker records

The minute books kept by the Religious Society of Friends (Quakers) record births, marriages, deaths and burials and you can consult those up to 1841 at the National Archives, and similar records up to 1837, by contacting the Society in London.

Births:
Date and place of birth, the child's and parents' names (and, very useful this, occasionally the grandparents' names) and the father's occupation.

Marriages:
Date, the couple's names and addresses, the man's occupation, the names and addresses of the couple's fathers and a list of their relations and other Friends who witnessed the happy event.

Deaths and burials:
Date, name and address, age, occupation and quite often the deceased's parents.

Welsh naming traditions

You'll find that surnames follow a different pattern in the earlier Welsh parish registers and this can be summed up in one word 'patronymics'; (it can be summed up in two words if you're counting the word 'confusing'). Instead of a fixed surname, each person was given their father's forename as their surname. For example: Thomas Morgan might be the son of Morgan Rees, and Morgan Rees, the son of Rees Griffith.

The ecclesiastical census

This tip is useful for locating a non-conformist chapel. In 1851 a country-wide census was taken of all places of worship. The census, arranged by county, was to include the address of every church, chapel or meeting house, the date each was built or founded, and the size of the congregation. The bad news is, the census isn't always complete for each district, but it's worth searching the County Archives copies.

Do you ken your Scottish kin?

Children in Scotland were named according to certain customs. Here's my tip to help you identify those Scottish ancestors.

- The first son was named after his paternal grandfather.
- The second son, after his maternal grandfather.
- The third son got his own father's name.
- The first daughter was named after her maternal grandmother.
- The second daughter, after her paternal grandmother.
- The third daughter got her own mother's name.

Don't confuse your in-laws with your steps!

We all know the difference between a stepmother and a mother-in-law – there aren't so many jokes about stepmothers for one thing! But up until the early 19th century the term 'in-law' was used for both, so this is something you might need to bear in mind when sorting out family relationships.

All change – or not …

The changeover from patronymics to fixed surnames took place from the early 1700s to the mid 1800s, with the decision to abandon the old system often dependant on how close they lived to their English neighbours! Not only that, but some Welsh clergy continued to record details in the parish registers using patronymics even when the families had stopped! So if you can't find an entry using the surname, try again using the patronymic name.

Quick tip

JOINED TOGETHER – DIFFERENT NAMES
Another thing that often crops up in the older Welsh parish records is the practice of referring to a married woman by her maiden name, so don't let it throw you if for example you come across: Margaret Lewis, the wife of William Rees.

Three reasons why a child might have an alias

Some children are listed with aliases (James Smith alias Jones) and this can usually be accounted for in one of three ways.

1. The child is illegitimate.
2. The parents' marriage took place in a non-conformist chapel.
3. A widow remarried and the child is part of a stepfamily.

Perusing the Parish records
Chapter summary:

- Use the Bishop's Transcripts when the parish registers are hard to read.

- Couples married in a parish where one of them resided.

- A marriage licence lists two guarantors – often other family members.

- A burial may be in an ancestor's place of birth, not where they died.

- Check Anglican parish registers for con-conformist burials.

- Cemeteries have separate internment registers.

- Locate non-conformist chapels on the ecclesiastical census.

- Scottish naming customs mostly followed a particular pattern.

- Familiarise yourself with Welsh patronymic naming.

- Stepfamily members were once called 'in-laws'.

"Some family trees have beautiful leaves, and some have just a bunch of nuts. Remember, it is the nuts that make the tree worth shaking."

Anon

Delving into
the archives

"A great place to start your family tree."

chapter 4
Delving into the archives

Did you know that The National Archives (NA) in Kew (originally called The Public Record Office), houses all government records over a certain age and holds the largest collection of information about individuals and households during the 19th century?

The National Archives **www.thenationalarchives.gov.uk**

County Archives (still sometimes known as a record office) hold records for that particular county and is where you'll find the parish registers and census returns. The huge variety of records held at these local archives means you'll be spoilt for choice and they include things like wills and probate records, old newspapers and journals, Quarter Sessions records, Poor Law records, non-conformist registers, tithe maps, electoral registers and manorial records.

Local reference libraries also hold some genealogical gems: maps, censuses, newspapers, and lots of other useful documents.

DID YOU KNOW ...

Some 6,800 miles of railway track had been laid by navvies in Britain between 1829 and 1851. But farmers weren't happy; they believed that trains would cause their cows to miscarry.

Be prepared

If you're planning a trip to The National Archives, here are a few tips worth knowing before your visit.

1. You'll be issued with a reader's ticket so remember to take some ID with you – a UK driving licence, credit card, cheque book or passport, are all acceptable.
2. Take a notebook or ring binder. You're allowed to take up to 20 loose sheets of paper into the reading rooms.
3. Equip yourself with pencils, as pens are not allowed.
4. Some areas of the reading rooms have points for laptops.
5. Digital photography is allowed in some areas.
6. Mobile phones must be turned to silent mode but can be used to take photographs.

Three things to do – before you visit Kew

The sheer volume and range of material held at the NA is mind-boggling so, to make sure you don't come out of there feeling you know less than when you went in, use this checklist before your visit.

- Write down what you already know and what you want to explore further.
- Check the online catalogue to see what records might be relevant to you and the sort of information they contain.
- Make a list of the documents you think will help you and copy down their location and reference numbers.

There are more
than ten million
original documents
in the care of the
National Archives.

Order documents in advance

Save time by ordering documents before you visit the National Archives. Choose what you want from the online catalogue and order the documents using the 'Request this' facility, or give them a ring. The documents will be produced the same day if the request is made during document ordering hours.

ANOTHER TIME-SAVING TIP
The NA allows you to view a maximum of 21 items a day. Because it can take anything up to 45 minutes to produce documents for each searcher, it's a really good idea to order several at the same time – usually you're allowed to request three in one go.

Coming to a Family History Centre near you!

If you can't get to the National Archives in Kew, all may not be lost. A lot of their records are available on microfilm and microfiche and you can hire them in at a Family History Centre by paying a small monthly or quarterly fee. These Centres are run by members of the Church of Jesus Christ of Latter-day Saints, so check their website to see if there's one near you. **www.familysearch.org**

> **DID YOU KNOW ...**
> The last public hanging was in 1868.

Family Records Centre

The FRC in Islington, London doesn't hold any original documents, but here you can access lots of essential filmed copies and indexed digital images, from census returns to wills. Coach parties and group visits are welcome at the Centre, so round up a few family history buddies and take a genealogy jaunt! **www.familyrecords.gov.uk/frc**

The National Library of Wales

The NLW is the archive centre for researching your Welsh genealogy. The collections include thousands of documents, photographs and pictures, maps and sound recordings. The resources are available free of charge but you'll need a reader's ticket to access the Reading Rooms. You need to take two proofs of identity, at least one showing your present address, and two passport size photos. There's an application form on their website at: **www.llgc.org.uk**

Web checks

It's practically unheard of now for a County Archives office or a library not to have a website. So before you spend time and money travelling to these places, check online for any descriptions of the records they hold, their policies regarding access or restrictions to documents and any charges they make. Opening times, telephone numbers, email addresses, and a location map are usually included, too.

How to avoid the 'lost sheep' look

County Archives usually produce their own information leaflets, so request these before your visit. The leaflets give a general overview of what records are available and how the particular system works at each office. They'll often include a plan of the reading room, so you'll already have a fair idea of where various documents are kept before you get there.

Picture this …

Collections of original photographs and old picture postcards are held in County Archives and reference libraries. See if they have anything that might be connected to your own research – village scenes are particularly useful and might show your ancestor's home, or even your ancestor!

Directory enquiry

Most County Archives and libraries hold a collection of local trade directories as well as directories published for specialist occupations and some of these can date back 200 years or more. These directories were originally produced for the bigger cities, but there's usually a good selection for smaller towns and counties. In the early ones the names and addresses of many tradesmen are listed and in the later ones private householders were added. So let your fingers do the walking and try a bit of ancestor name spotting!

The professionals!

If your ancestor was in one of the professions, look in a directory of its members or fellows. A directory published in the right time period will sometimes supply useful biographical info such as academic training, how members progressed in their careers and even their addresses.

To the manor born ...

Manorial records can go back to the 13th century, though unfortunately most of those before 1733 are written in Latin. Found in County Archives, the manorial rolls and books contain reports on the twice-yearly meetings of the Lord of the Manor or Court Baron and all the manor's ongoing shenanigans! Discover when tenants' land changed hands, where the land was situated, its size, and annual rent. Other useful manorial records are the half-yearly rent books and rolls, which name tenants, their property and the rent due.

Upstairs, downstairs, in the County Archives!

Large households usually meant domestic servants, and a record of wages paid to these people would have been kept in an account book. Many of these household inventories have been deposited in local archives, so these are worth looking out for if your ancestor was someone who worked 'below stairs' as a butler, cook, maid, coachman, or gardener.

Ancestors behaving badly

More serious crimes were heard by a Justice of the Peace at the Quarter Sessions. If one of your forebears committed a crime there are various records you can consult at County Archives; these include things like:

- Rolls and papers – which give details of individual cases.
- Minute books.
- Lists of prisoners.

I beg your pardon!

Thousands of Britons left for the colonies – though not always willingly! After 1615, things began to look up for prisoners and those who might once have been faced with a death sentence were often transported overseas instead. The National Archives hold a book by Peter Wilson Coldham called The Complete Book of Emigrants in Bondage, 1614-1775, which gives a list of convicts transported during this time and where they were tried.

Was your ancestor
one of the twelve good men?

In 1825, only men aged between 21 and 60 could serve on a jury and lists of jurors can be found with Quarter Sessions records at County Archives. But they couldn't be just anyone; they needed to fulfil certain criteria. They had to have owned property worth at least £10 a year, leased property worth at least £20 a year or rented property worth at least £30 a year.

For less serious crimes ...

Drunkenness and similar lapses weren't considered major crimes and were dealt with by the local magistrate at petty, county or borough sessions. Registers of the cases heard at these courts are now mostly held at County Archives.

Transportation

The National Archives hold registers of convicts transported to New South Wales and Van Diemen's Land (renamed Tasmania in 1856) from 1787 to 1870 and these are listed by ships' name and departure dates. The details include; prisoners' names, ages, the date and place of the trial, the offence committed, and the length of the sentence.

> **DID YOU KNOW ...**
> Wealthy people were often buried inside the church.

Gaol house roll!

Gaol calendars don't depict saucy shots of prisoners, but what they do reveal are interesting facts about those detained in the county lockup! Found in the County Archives, the calendars list:

- Names, ages and occupations of prisoners.
- The alleged crime.
- The verdict and sentence handed out.

A career in the army?

Ask if your nearest reference library has a copy of the Army Lists if a member of your family was a commissioned officer in the British Army. The Lists were printed quarterly from 1879 to 1950 (and annually between 1754 and 1879), and can widen your knowledge of an ancestor's army career.

Did your ancestors migrate to Britain?

The Aliens Act of 1793 meant that all foreigners arriving in Britain had to supply certain information to official bodies. Migrants already resident, and householders where they'd taken up lodgings, were required to give details of name, rank or occupation, and address to a local magistrate or a parish overseer and these declarations are likely to be held at County Archives.

DID YOU KNOW ...
No census was taken in 1941, when Britain was at war.

Read all about it!

If you have the opportunity (and stacks of time to spare) then a library that serves your ancestor's district can be the best place for browsing copies of vintage newspapers for a reference to their death. My tip is to look for ...

An obituary or death notice: these could supply you with added background information such as who attended the funeral and who the closest relatives were. It might also help you identify other family connections by giving names and their relationship to the deceased.

Reports of sudden death: stories of sudden deaths are often featured in local newspapers and might help solve a mystery for you. If one of your ancestors died young it might have been the result of an accident and so is quite likely to have been reported on.

Lost the plot?

Luckily, records have been kept of where people are buried and these will provide you with names, dates, and burial plot numbers. Once you have an idea of where your ancestor was buried, get in touch with the local council who'll have phone numbers for the municipal cemeteries in that area. County Archives will have contact details for individual churchwardens if you think your ancestor was buried in a churchyard.

Written in stone …

… or not, as the case may be! Gravestones, especially older ones, have a nasty habit of becoming worn and illegible, but, with a lot of patience, you can often pick out enough of the wording to piece together some interesting data. The really clever tip here is to see if anyone has already done this laborious task for you. Family History Societies produce many useful booklets and CDs, including ones on monumental inscriptions.

Tracing ancestors

Most County Archives offices have a photocopying rule or two. Usually a document which is too big, too fragile, or has a wax seal is a definite no-no. My tip is to take along a digital camera for photographing documents and some tracing paper for copying any relevant details from maps.

Quick tip

PHOTO FINISH

Do a trial run of your digital photographing techniques on some documents at home before attempting the real thing in the archives environment. Try your camera at different settings and at different distances from the document and check that the results are readable on screen and when printed out.

Delving into the archives
Chapter summary:

- Some form of ID is required when visiting archive offices.
- Check archives' websites and online catalogues.
- Save time by ordering documents before you visit Kew.
- Look up your nearest Family History Centre.
- Professional and trade directories are valuable resources.
- Remember the County Archives' biographical section.
- Helpful documents are found amongst the Quarter Sessions records.
- Search newspapers for obituaries and death notices.
- Family History Societies publish monumental inscriptions.
- Practise taking digital photos of documents.

"Search out the past ...
know yourself ...
look to the future. "

Anon

Widening the net

chapter 5
Widening the net

With more and more genealogical data becoming available on the Internet, you might be in serious danger of information overload! So here are my top tips for using some of the best resources on the Web and what you might expect from them.

International Genealogical Index (IGI)

The IGI is a massive index of baptisms and marriages covering the years from 1838 to around 1875 compiled by the Church of Jesus Christ of Latter-day Saints. The majority of entries on the index are taken from Anglican parish registers with some taken from Baptist, Methodist and Independent registers but fewer from Quakers, Jews and Catholic sources.
www.familysearch.org

Building blocks

Give the IGI a shot if you don't know your ancestor's parish as the entry will give you this information. Tracking someone down this way means you can now search the relevant parish registers for all those other family details. You'll be able to:

- Find where your ancestor was baptised (and probably born).

- Track them down if they moved from one place to another.

- Locate the parish where a couple married (usually where the woman lived).

Come out, wherever you are!

You'd think that somewhere amongst the millions of names listed on the IGI they'd have the one you're looking for wouldn't you? But don't be too surprised if your ancestor proves to be illusive because, although data has been used from every country, none of the indexes is actually complete. So use the IGI as a guide only.

When things don't add up

The IGI is a terrific thing but like a lot of resources it does contain a number of discrepancies. This is because the indexes are a mixture of details taken from the primary sources and data supplied by private individuals, and things don't always tally with what's found in the parish registers. So be sure to bear this in mind and always double-check the information you find in the IGI with that in the actual parish register.

Documents Online

This site gives you almost more family history documents than you can shake a stick at! Searching the digitised index won't cost you a penny, but there's a small charge to view an image. If you use this resource at the National Archives or the Family History Centre, viewing the images is free, but you pay for any copies you take.
www.nationalarchives.gov.uk/documentsonline

The ancestry website

Some of the records are only accessible to subscribers, but you can view the complete UK General Register Office indexes of births, marriages, and deaths here free of charge – which is why this website is not only invaluable, but also one of my personal favourites. The GRO resource is fully searchable, with over 250 million names and covers the years from 1837 to 1983.

The England and Wales census data on Ancestry (1841 to 1901) shows images of the original records and can be viewed on a 'pay per view' or 'pay per voucher' system.

There's a free index for the 1881 England, Wales, Isle of Man, and Channel Islands census. If you locate one of your ancestors, click on the 'view record' symbol to see all the other family members living at the same address – very helpful.
www.ancestry.co.uk

Access to Archives

Not all the good stuff is held at the National Archives. Take a peek at the online catalogue at the Access to Archives website, 'A2A'; this lists the whereabouts and reference numbers of millions of other records that are kept in local archive centres in England and Wales. **www.a2a.org.uk**

DID YOU KNOW ...
The Education Act of 1880 meant going to school became mandatory for all 5-10 year olds.

Scotland's People

This is the official government source for Scottish genealogy. They have various charges to view the online documents, but there are almost 50 million of them! The site's data includes statutory registers (civil registration of births, marriages and deaths), old parish registers, wills, and censuses.
www.scotlandspeople.gov.uk

Moving Here

The Moving Here website is a good one to try if you know your ancestors were immigrants to England during the last 200 years. Resources include documents, photographs, and film clips. There's free access to an online catalogue relating to those from the Caribbean, Ireland, South Asia, and Jewish communities. **www.movinghere.org.uk**

Jewish Genealogical Society of Great Britain

The resources and databases here are useful for family historians who wish to trace their Jewish ancestors whether they came to the UK from overseas or left for pastures new.
www.jgsgb.org.uk

Library and Archives Canada

The searchable Home Children database has the names, ages, name of ship and year of arrival of over 100,000 British children who were sent to Canada during the child emigration movement between 1869 and 1930.
www.collectionscanada.ca

Family history societies online

Family history societies aren't just an online resource, but it's much simpler to locate the online presence of any particular society by going through the Federation of Family History Societies website. The Federation's site has details of regional societies in England, Wales, and Ireland listed alphabetically by county. Also included on their website are overseas societies in Australia, Canada, New Zealand, and the USA. **www.ffhs.org.uk**

Family history societies and local connections

Each individual family history society focuses on the genealogy of a specific region and it can be well worth signing up for membership in order to gain some insider know-how. Members collate heaps of local data, and these transcripts are available to other members or sold in booklets or on CD-ROM. The size and activity of family history societies vary, but their research databases include things like:

- Local surname lists.
- Various census indexes.
- Burial indexes.
- Some indexes to regional institutions.
- Monumental inscriptions.
- War memorials.
- Local police service records.
- Quarter Sessions.

Guild of One-Name Studies

This is a UK based organisation that welcomes new members. With some 7,000 surnames on their list, it's possible that someone has already taken the hard work out of researching your family name. Every one of the surnames is registered by a member who collects information worldwide and there's an easy to use search facility on their website.
www.one-name.org

Contact Guild members ...

You don't need to be a member of the Guild of One-Name Studies yourself in order to contact its members. Guild members are under an obligation to answer any query, so long as you pay the postage.

- If you live in the same country as the member you wish to contact, send an SAE with your query.
- If you live in a different country you'll need to send three International Reply Coupons in lieu of stamps.
- If you contact them by email you won't have to pay anything!

Not all of the Guild's members have their contact details displayed on the website but they are included on a printed register, which is available through the site.

DID YOU KNOW ...
The formal adoption of children came into force in 1927.

What to ask …

If you're contacting one of the Guild members you'll get much better results if you can be specific about what you want to know. But don't overload them with information – sending your entire family history isn't a good idea!

1. Give details of the names you're looking into – the maiden name of a spouse can help distinguish someone with a common surname.

2. Provide any information you have regarding dates.

3. The location is important, so give details about any place your ancestors settled.

One-name studies can take years to put together and Guild members amass huge amounts of data. Their research is ongoing with facts constantly awaiting validation, so the biggest no-no when approaching one of them is to ask them for 'everything you have on so and so'!

Historical directories

This is a handy website to visit if you want to look up your ancestor's professional career: **www.1837online.com**.

Not all of the professions are listed but you'll find those for:

- Some officers in the British Army.
- Dental surgery directory for 1925.
- Clergy list for 1896.
- Medical register for 1913.

A family business …

The National Register of Archives has a website which is a database of details concerning family and business papers. The search facility allows you to explore by family or personal name, corporate name or place name and gives information about the dates and whereabouts of individual records. **www.nationalarchives.gov.uk/nra**

Hospital corner

With this database you can search for the location of specific hospital records in the UK. Be warned though that most hospital records are subject to closure periods (often 100 years) and access to an individual's records is not normally allowed. My tip would be to talk to the archivist at the repository before you visit, to see what might actually be available to you. **www.nationalarchives.gov.uk/hospitalrecords**

Back to basics

Someone (probably) once said that a document was only as accurate as the person who transcribed it. Whenever possible try to view the original data and avoid the scribes' version of Chinese Whispers! Lots of websites now have scanned copies of original documents posted online and this is the next best thing to seeing records in person.

> **DID YOU KNOW …**
> In Scotland, divorce could be granted from 1560.

No place like home

If you have access to the Internet at home, do as much of your preliminary research as possible from the comfort of your own swivel chair. A lot of the background information you need to gather can be found online, thus enabling you to spend your time at the various archives studying the original sources that aren't available on the Web.

Using keywords

Searching for information on some genealogy websites is like looking for the proverbial needle in a haystack with thousands of possible results throwing themselves at you. So where the facility is offered, use the advanced or refined search boxes to narrow things down. These usually require a date range or location, or a keyword. But as not all 'keywords' will be listed in the document index or catalogue you will end up with limited results. My tip is to search using name, date, and location first, and then try various keywords if the search brings up too many results to trawl through.

> **DID YOU KNOW ...**
> During WW2 around 80 per cent of married women, and 90 per cent of single women, were involved in some kind of war work.

Gin was one of the
most popular drinks
in the 17th century,
and it's estimated
that Britons were
consuming 8,000,000
gallons a year.

And finally: hiring a researcher

It's unlikely there'll ever be a time when all genealogical records are available online so sooner or later you'll need to consult documents in the flesh! When it isn't feasible to do this yourself, hiring a researcher is the next best thing. Here are my tips for choosing the right researcher for you.

1. Website content varies but a researcher should willingly offer advice and be able to tell you what records are held in their local area.

2. Ask them for a recommendation from a previous client, though understandably many are reluctant to ask clients to give out their email addresses to strangers.

3. Get the researcher to do a small amount of work for you before spending larger sums of money.

Widening the net
Chapter summary:

- Track down your ancestor's parish on the IGI.

- Remember that the IGI is not complete.

- The GRO indexes can be viewed on the Ancestry website.

- Locate the whereabouts of millions of documents at Access to Archives.

- Try the Moving Here website for immigrant ancestors to England.

- Find useful local databases at Family History Societies.

- Trace your surname through the Guild of One-Name Studies.

- Try the National Register of Archives for family and business papers.

- Always view original documents whenever practicable.

- Do as much as possible of your preliminary research from home.

"Why waste your money looking up your family tree? Just go into politics and your opponents will do it for you!

Mark Twain

Poor ancestors – rich pickings

chapter 6

chapter 6

Poor ancestors – rich pickings

Discovering you have a poor ancestor or two in your family tree could be to your advantage, even if it wasn't to theirs! Poor Law records are one of the richest sources available to family historians and can be found at the relevant County Archives.

Up until 1834, each parish was a self-governing body and accountable for its own poor. This meant the wealthier folk of the parish paid money into the poor rate to help their less fortunate neighbours. This poor rate was collected and administered by the parish officers (overseers and churchwardens).

So from apprentices to workhouses, here are my top tips for finding out how things really were!

DID YOU KNOW ...
Around 30,000 children were sent to the British colonies and the USA at the beginning of WW2, to ensure their safety.

The overseers' accounts

The detailed account books kept by the parish overseers are chock full of valuable information so should be near the top of your 'resources to search' list. The overseers' accounts date mostly from the 18th and 19th centuries and name those who were in need of poor relief, what was provided, and how much it cost. Here's a list of just some of those things:

- House rent – the amount and how often it was paid.
- Fuel.
- Essential clothing.
- Food.
- Ale.
- Medicines.
- Money paid to someone who nursed the sick.
- Coffins and shrouds.

Quick tip

SURVIVING THE HARD TIMES
You might still find something about your family in the Poor Law records even if they weren't generally considered to be paupers. Ordinary families sometimes found themselves in reduced circumstances and unable to work due to injury or ill health.

Legally settled or legal settlement?

Here's a confusing one! You'll find references to poor ancestors in the overseers' accounts of their place of legal settlement, which won't necessarily be the parish where they chose to live. Plenty of people lived in one parish but were required to seek aid from another.

So what is this place of legal settlement?

From around 1662 to 1834, everyone had a place of legal settlement – though this could be different from their place of birth.

Legal settlement particularly affected the poor and here's why: being responsible for their own people, the parish officers weren't too happy about supporting 'outsiders' so if anyone looked like they might become a burden on the parish coffers, for whatever reason, they were often dispatched back to their own legal settlement pretty sharpish.

Settlement and illegitimate children

Legitimate children automatically took their father's place of settlement, even if they were born somewhere else. But illegitimate children could claim a legal settlement in the place they were born. This led to many a pregnant girl being returned post haste to her own settlement!

DID YOU KNOW …
Transportation of criminals formally ended in 1867.

Removal orders

These were the legal documents used to send someone back to their place of settlement. They often give helpful information about those being removed, including the names of spouses and dependent children.

Down on their luck

Another interesting set of papers, found amongst the Quarter Sessions cases, are those dealing with vagrancy. These examinations give name, age, parish of birth, and spouse's name. 'Vagrant' covered a multitude of situations and could be any number of things:

- Women whose husbands had abandoned them.
- People who had become ill while journeying.
- Discharged soldiers and their families.
- Apprentices who had run away from cruel masters.

A minute in the vestry!

If you've passed on the Vestry Minutes believing they have rather less to do with family history than with the welfare of the vicar's vestments, think again! Each Easter, this was where the parish officers were elected and the yearly poor rate decided. Discussions regarding the parish poor were the main topic at these regular powwows, so my tip is to check these out.

Indenture adventure

Orphans and children of poorer families were often apprenticed. The masters were sometimes 'chosen' by the parish officers and weren't always any happier about the situation than the children! Two indentures were signed and one was handed to the apprentice when his apprenticeship was completed. If you find one of these indentures it'll give you the following info.

- The name and age of the apprentice.
- The name of the apprentice's parents.
- The trade the apprentice learned.
- The apprentice's parish.
- The master's name and occupation.

Youth initiative!

An apprentice could be anything from 7 to 21 years old and some were undoubtedly used simply as a source of cheap labour. The overseers' accounts books might show a record of payment made to a local farmer or householder who'd taken in a child.

Illegitimate children in the Quarter Sessions Records

If a couple didn't marry, a case against the putative father might be brought to the Quarter Sessions. These useful 'bastardy documents' will give you the father's name and place of residence. A good tip here: the Sessions are comprised of files and minute books – look for the relevant case in the minute books first and save heaps of time.

Children in the workhouse were required to have a minimum of three hours schooling a day.

Examination after birth

A formal examination could be made after an illegitimate child was born. This was a sworn statement made by the mother before a Justice of the Peace and reveals the father's name, place of residence and occupation, and shows whether the child was male or female.

Bastardy Bonds

These were documents signed by fathers of illegitimate children agreeing to a maintenance payment until the child was seven years old. They were used quite often in the 17th and 18th centuries to release the parish from financial responsibility. A Bastardy Bond relating to one of your ancestors will often give you the name of the man's father too, as it's likely he stood as one of the Bond's guarantors.

Quick tip

ANOTHER WAY TO DISCOVER A FATHER'S IDENTITY ...
The overseer kept a careful tally of incomings and outgoings in his accounts book. This included payments made to mothers of illegitimate children and money collected from reputed fathers.

DID YOU KNOW ...
In 1864, a new law forbad boys less than ten years of age from working as chimney sweeps.

Workhouse rules

It wasn't compulsory to stay in the workhouse but if a man left of his own accord, his family had to leave too. Some admission and discharge registers are held in local archives and are a useful place to look if you think your ancestor might have spent some time in a workhouse. These registers give the names, ages, addresses, religion, and dates of admission and discharge for each inmate.

Finding ancestors who died in the workhouse

When workhouse inmates died, their burials were often taken care of by family outside, and records of these are usually found in the family's parish church. When this didn't happen, the workhouse Board of Guardians arranged burial locally in unmarked graves, so search the parish register where the workhouse was situated too.

Auctioning a pauper's property

Sometimes an overseer sold off a pauper's possessions in the hope of making back the money the parish had paid out in poor relief. Records of these sales might show up in the overseers' accounts or occasionally in the Quarter Sessions records.

DID YOU KNOW ...
The word 'bridegroom' is a corruption of the Old English word 'brydguma' (bride man).

Poor ancestors – rich pickings
Chapter summary:

- Overseers' Accounts are full of valuable information.
- Many ordinary families claimed from the poor rate.
- At one time, everyone was assigned a 'place of legal settlement'.
- Removal orders often give details of whole families.
- The Vestry Minutes record useful poor law business.
- Apprentice indentures can offer further leads.
- Quarter Sessions records may contain details of illegitimate children.
- An Examination after birth reveals details of an illegitimate child's father.
- Workhouse records are held at County Archives.
- Overseers sometimes sold a pauper's possessions in an auction.

"What the next generation will value most is not what we owned, but the evidence of who we were and the tales of how we loved. In the end, it's the family stories that are worth the storage.

Ellen Goodman

Worldly goods & chattels

THE LAST WILL &
TESTAMENT OF
LORD HAZELMERE

chapter 7
Worldly goods & chattels

While researching your family history you might discover the last will and testament of a wealthy ancestor and this document can reveal all sorts of things about him. But it wasn't only wealthy people who made wills – even those with few belongings to leave often had strong opinions about who should get them!

There are plenty of hints you can pick up about your family's past from other documents, too. The following tips will help you learn more about your ancestors' property, possessions and standard of living.

Get your free wills index here!

The registered copies of PCC wills from 1384 to 1858 have been indexed and are available online. This is a particularly easy one to search and, for a small charge, will even take you to a digital image of the will.

www.nationalarchives.gov.uk/documentsonline

DID YOU KNOW ...
By the middle of the 19th century, around two thirds of children from working class backgrounds regularly attended Sunday school.

Where there's a will …

Before the civil probate registries came into being in 1858, wills were proved in church courts; the main ones in England and Wales being the Prerogative Court of York (PCY), which dealt with the northern dioceses and the Prerogative Court of Canterbury (PCC), which dealt with the southern ones. These are the ones to check if your ancestor was reasonably well-heeled. But those with less to leave might have had their will proved in a lower court.

- Wills proved in the PCC from 1384 until 1858 are held at the National Archives.
- Wills proved in the PCY from 1389 until 1858 are held at the Borthwick Institute of Historical Research, York.
- Wills proved in lower courts are usually held in County Archives.
- Wills proved in the Welsh ecclesiastical courts from 1521 until 1858 are at the National Library of Wales, Aberystwyth.

Willing suspension!

If you have a burial date, you'll probably be thinking that it makes sense to use this as a starting point when searching for a will — and you'd be right. But wills weren't always proved within six months of a person's death, so you might need to search longer than you thought. Work forward from the burial date for up to 15 years.

For later wills ...

It gets simpler (sort of). From the beginning of 1858, wills in England and Wales were proved either in the Principal Probate Registry at High Holborn, London or at a District Probate Registry (full list on their website). There are indexes from 1858 to date at High Holborn, where you can also order document copies. **www.hmcourts-service.gov.uk/cms/wills.htm**

The National Archives and the Family Records Centre have copies of the annual indexes to 1943 but if you live in the relevant district ask at the County Archives or reference library as most of them also have these indexes.

Women's wills

Before the Married Women Property Act of 1882, women's possessions belonged to their husbands. This was not only a pretty raw deal but means wills made by married women are as rare as hen's teeth. But look for wills made by widows and spinsters because these can be revealing. If they had no children of their own, they probably left bequests to their own siblings, or to their nephews and nieces.

Grant of probate

If you come across an ancestor's will, you'll find it consists of two documents — the will and the grant of probate. The will itself is usually considered to be the interesting bit, specifying how the testator's possessions should be doled out, but the probate grant can be very informative too. Look out for a date, the executors' names and relationship to the deceased, and the value of the estate.

You've had your share!

Sometimes people distributed their worldly goods before they died; handing over property to a son or bestowing a marriage settlement on a daughter for instance. If one of the deceased's children has been left a measly sum in a will – often a shilling – this token legacy usually indicates an earlier settlement on that child rather than a family fall out!

But who got his land?

There were two types of land ownership and two reasons why your ancestor's land might not be mentioned in his will. Any copyhold land was ultimately held by the manor and couldn't be transferred to another person without a lot of rigmarole and the say-so of the manorial court. Freehold land automatically passed to the nearest blood relative – with sons and male descendants first in line.

Scottish wills

For wills of those north of the border, visit the Scotland's People website where you can search the indexes of more than 611,000 entries to wills and testaments (probate documents) from 1513-1901, free of charge. The index doesn't tell you the names of executors, trustees or heirs to the estate. Nor will you learn the deceased's date of death, or the value of the estate.

Scottish wills and testaments can give you the forename, surname, occupation, and place of residence of the deceased, the court in which the testament was recorded, and the date.
www.scotlandspeople.gov.uk

Quick tip

FOR LOYAL SERVICE ...
Was one of your forebears a servant 'up at the big 'ouse'?
If they were, the master – or mistress – might have
mentioned them in his, or her, will. Loyalty was often
rewarded with a small (sometimes very small) sum.

Next of kin please step forward ...

Even if your ancestor didn't leave a will, you might still be
able to find something called a bond of administration (or
admon). This was a legal document that gave the next of kin
the authority to dispose of any property belonging to their
late lamented nearest and dearest!

Personal possessions

A will usually mentions personal possessions only if these were
left to someone specifically, but a probate inventory is often
more revealing about your ancestor. An inventory will list their
belongings, often room by room, and include stuff like furniture,
tools, clothing and so on.

DID YOU KNOW ...
There were 133,514 officers and men in the British Army
in 1914.

Intestacy and who got what …

When a man died without leaving a will, his personal estate was distributed according to a certain pecking-order.

1. His wife got one third.
2. His legitimate children got the rest, divided equally between them. They also got their mother's share if she was already dead.
3. Grandchildren got their parent's share if that parent had died.
4. The deceased's parents.
5. The deceased's aunts and uncles (or their children).

Estate papers

The Estate accounts books of a local bigwig could give you some information about any property or land your forebear rented. These papers, often to be discovered in the County Archives, give names of all the estate tenants, what they were renting, and how much they paid.

Rental records

If someone in your family line rented a property from an organisation or a charity, the County Archives might well hold records of the tenancy. Chances are you will already have a good idea of where they were living from searching the parish registers and census returns. The types of property you could look out for include:

- An almshouse.
- A school house.
- A parsonage.

After the Act of 1666, it was a legal requirement that all bodies be buried wrapped in nothing but woollen cloth.

Good deeds

Lots of old property deeds have survived, even if the buildings themselves have fallen down. A search in the County Archives that covers the area in which your ancestor lived could prove very useful in your family research. These deeds will indicate the location of the property your ancestor owned and will also give some details of its size. Whether your ancestor was buying or selling the property, other names will appear on the document and these could indicate other family members.

A Marriage Settlement

Some husbands presented their new brides with a settlement of money or property before the marriage took place. This legal document meant the lucky lady was entitled to a lifetime interest and could bequeath the money or property to her children in her will. The downside was that often the Marriage Settlement laid down rules of how much of her new-found wealth she'd be entitled to should she be widowed! Surviving Marriage Settlements are held in County Archives.

> **DID YOU KNOW ...**
> Men, known as Bevan Boys, were conscripted to work in the mines from 1943.

The Hearth Tax

Some people would tax anything! The one levied on hearths at 2 shillings per hearth was as unpopular as the rest, but hey, the King had to live on something. Payable by the occupier rather than the owner of a property, those whose house was worth less than 20 shillings (£1) in annual rent were exempt. The Hearth Tax period was from 1662 to 1689 though not all records survive. They record both chargeable and non-chargeable households and are the nearest you'll get to a national census before the 19th century. The National Archives hold the originals, but many County Archives have transcripts.

Land Tax records

This tax, with its annual listing of names, was brought in during the late 17th century, but for family historians the lists made between 1780 and 1832 could yield some interesting results. During these years the Clerks of the Peace used the roll as a means of determining those who could vote in parliamentary elections. You'll find the Land Tax records mostly in County Archives in the Quarter Sessions collections – they provide names of owners and tenants of houses and land, and often include the names of the property too.

The parish ratepayers

People might have considered themselves fortunate to have money, but a lot less lucky when the rate bill dropped on the mat! The Churchwardens' Accounts give a list of parishioners who contributed each year towards the poor rate, and the sum each paid.

Try the tithe maps

A tithe was a payment made by parishioners to support the parish church and its clergy, and if your ancestor owned land he would have handed over his tithe payment with the rest. Originally this was a tenth of the yearly produce of the land and paid in kind (wool, milk, crops, etc) but an Act in 1836 required that the payment be made in the form of a rent-charge. A survey of the whole of England and Wales took place and the tithe maps (held in County Archives) are the result, showing the boundaries of land and the acreage of fields.

The tithe apportionments

The apportionments, with plot numbers matching those on the tithe maps, are the really useful half of the tithe double-act, and supply all sorts of information.

- The name of the landowner.
- The occupier.
- The name of the property or land.
- The amount of rent-charge payable.
- The acreage.
- The state of cultivation: pasture, orchard, arable, garden and so on.

DID YOU KNOW ...
Between 1777 and 1852 in Britain, there was a tax on households that employed male servants.

Worldly goods and chattels
Chapter summary:

- A will might not have been proved for up to 15 years after a death.

- Look for a bond of administration if your ancestor didn't leave a will.

- Probate inventories are often more revealing than wills.

- Marriage settlements were quite common.

- Estate papers will list the names of tenants.

- The County Archives hold many old property deeds.

- The Hearth Tax is the nearest thing to a 19th century census.

- Land Tax records provide names of owners and occupiers.

- Churchwardens' Accounts list those who contributed to the poor rate.

- Tithe apportionments give details about landowners and tenants.

A man who thinks
too much about
his ancestors is like a
potato – the best part
of him is underground.

Henry S. F. Cooper

Calendars &
dates & spelling,
oh my!

chapter 8
Calendars & dates & spelling, oh my!

As if you didn't have enough to do tracing all those ancestors back in time and deciphering all that undecipherable handwriting, you're now expected to learn a whole new language – well, almost! Once you set foot in the 1700s you'll be sure to come across documents written in Latin, and you'll also need to take into account a calendar change. Use my tips for making sense of these records, and bluff your way out of trouble!

How times change!

In England, under the old style Julian calendar, each year began on 25th March. But by 1751 this calendar was incorrect by 11 days. Parliament decided England should keep up with the times (sorry!) and change to the new style Gregorian calendar (Scotland had already done this in 1660). Your ancestors' dates and ages might seem confusing if you don't allow for this changeover. Here's how it works:

1. The start of 1751 was on 25th March.

2. The year of 1751 ended on 31st December.

3. The new year of 1752 began on 1st January and ended 31st December.

4. In September of 1752, 11 days were taken out, so that 2nd September is directly followed by 14th September.

Short and sweet

In some of the older parish registers the clergymen – to save all that arduous writing – recorded the names of months in a sort of shorthand: 8ber, 9ber, and so on. These will be referring to the pre-Gregorian calendar months, so 8ber is the old October, and not the present day August.

Those Roman numerals!

There were also quite a few clergy with a penchant for Roman numerals, which makes the early parish registers less than easy going. Make things easier for yourself by keeping a note of the basics and you'll never again be left scratching your head!

- M = 1000
- D = 500
- C = 100
- L = 50
- X = 10
- V = 5
- I = 1

So the year MDCCLXXXVIII = 1788

DID YOU KNOW ...
Headstones weren't used in churchyards until the 17th century.

And those Latin dates!

A lot of the dates in older parish registers are written in Latin, but you might surprise yourself at just how many of these words you recognise – or be able to make a shrewd stab at.

- On the first = primo
- On the second = secundo
- On the third = tertio
- On the fourth = quarto
- On the fifth = quinto
- On the sixth = sexto
- On the seventh = septimo
- On the eighth = octavo
- On the ninth = nono
- On the tenth = decimo

Quick tip

GRAVE MISTAKES

Be careful that the wording on an old tombstone doesn't trip you up. If you come upon a memorial where the inscription is clear enough to read, you might find it says something like 'died in his 40th year'. This phrasing was commonly used, and means he hadn't yet reached 40, but died at 39.

Latin lingo

Archivists are generally an obliging bunch, and there's usually at least one on duty at each County Archives office to help with those deciphering dilemmas! But as with the Latin numbers, a lot of the words used – this time for baptisms, marriages, and burials – will be instantly recognisable.

Baptisms:
Look for similar words like baptizat, baptizatus, baptizata or for words that sound like natal; renatus (reborn).

Marriages:
Anything that looks like matrimony or nuptials is a safe bet; matrimonium or nupsit for example.

Burials:
This time look out for words similar to sepulchre or mortuary such as sepultat or mortuus.

Oh no, more Latin!

Hold on, I'm nearly done. Here are seven (almost) painless ways to sort out who's who.

1. Filia = daughter
2. Filius = son
3. Uxor = wife
4. Relicta = widow
5. Vir = husband
6. Mater/pater = mother/father
7. Spurius = illegitimate

The name game

After 1733, most clergy did us all a great favour and stopped using Latin in the parish registers. Here's a tip to ensure this good news doesn't present you with a brand new puzzle.

Your ancestor's forename, written down the Latin way for a baptism pre-1733 and later changed to the English spelling for a marriage or burial entry, might cause you to think you're dealing with two different people.

Some Latinised names later became popular names in their own right, but it's their English equivalent that your ancestor would have been known by. Here are some popular ones:

- Maria – Mary
- Carolus – Charles
- Eliza – Elizabeth
- Gulielmus – William
- Jacobus – James
- Johanna – Joan
- Johannes – John

Decoding de handwriting

You're going to be coming across all kinds of handwriting, from the simple X to the ornate flourish with embellished twiddly bits. So here are three great interpreting tips.

1. The County Archives usually have books on handwriting styles covering various periods, or borrow one from your local library.

2. Use a magnifying glass and look closely at the handwriting you're trying to decipher. Pick out the letters, words and phrases you do recognise and compare these with the less legible ones.

3. I learned this trick some years ago: take a sheet of plain paper and, using a pencil, copy the document you want to decipher, leaving spaces where you're unsure of a word or letter. As the document takes shape many of the incomprehensible words become clear.

Write the dates right!

Another thing you need to remember is that not everyone writes date figures in the same order, which means you may be wrongly recording vital information, especially from websites. In Britain, the standard practice is writing day-month-year, while in the USA for example, it's month-day-year — so 1-12-1850 could be either the 1st December or January 12th.

> **DID YOU KNOW ...**
> The first workhouses were set up in the late 1600s.

Calendars & dates & spelling, oh my!

Chapter summary:

- Latin documents are common in the 1700s and beyond.
- The start of a new year was once 25th March.
- There was a major calendar change in 1751-52.
- Watch out for the clergymen's Latin shorthand.
- Make a note of the basic Roman numerals.
- Many Latin words are easily identifiable.
- Learn to recognise the Latin equivalent of popular names.
- Pick up a book on different handwriting styles.
- Date phrasing on old headstones can trip you up.
- The order in which day-month-year is written can vary.

Nothing is so soothing
to our self-esteem
as to find our bad
traits in our forebears.
It seems to absolve us.

Van Wyck Brooks

Thoroughly modern research!

chapter 9

chapter 9
Thoroughly modern research!

In genealogical terms, 'modern research' means anything less than a hundred years ago. But the time restrictions placed on a lot of modern records (often 50 or 100 years), means getting access to these documents can be very frustrating. Here are my top tips for researching some more recent family history.

Feel free to ask

The Freedom of Information Act came into effect in 2005, which means you can wave goodbye to the old standard 30-year closure period on data held by public authorities. As you might expect, exceptions to this rule apply to records containing personally sensitive or confidential information, but this doesn't always mean an absolute closure. Under the Freedom of Information Act, you can request information from 'closed' records by writing to the head archivist in charge of the relevant repository.

> **DID YOU KNOW ...**
> Between 1892 and 1954, around 12 million people entered the USA via the New York reception centre on Ellis Island.

The British Red Cross Society

From 1910, county branches of the British Red Cross were set up in the whole of the UK. If your ancestor was a member, County Archives might hold records which could include membership information. Local newspapers will also have reported on branch activities.

Show of hands

If you have a fairly good idea of your ancestor's address, you can take a look at the old electoral registers. In villages these are listed by surname, but in towns they're entered by street name. The County Archives or local library will hold the electoral registers for their own district. So who was eligible to vote?

1. By 1900 men aged 21 and over.
2. From 1900 women who were the sole owners of a house and therefore ratepayers (but only in local elections).
3. After 1918 women over 30 or those who were university graduates.
4. After 1918 woman who owned businesses or were the wives of extensive householders.
5. After 1928 women over 21.

If your ancestor was getting any kind of help from the Poor Law system they might have lost their vote.

In the club!

You might not remember Granddad as the 'get up and go' type, but in his sprightlier youth he might have belonged to one of the many rambling or cycling clubs (an old group photo with Gramps sporting a pair of knobbly knees and a bicycle is a dead giveaway here!). These sorts of clubs were often very efficiently run, and records of members and their club activities might be available in the County Archives or reports of them found in local newspapers archives.

Other popular pastimes ...

Early 20th century newspapers are full of snippets about clubs and societies, which will give you an inkling of what people did before telly was invented. Check out local archives for deposited records which might include:

- Choral society.
- Dramatic society.
- Beekeepers.
- Photographic society.
- Automobile clubs.
- Angling associations.
- Bible society.

Working on the railways

A multitude of different railway companies existed before nationalisation, employing many thousands of men and women – especially when the lines were being laid, and during the First World War. If a member of your family was once employed as a farm labourer, they might have been one of the many tempted away to work on local railway construction.

Over a quarter of a million under-age boys enlisted before 1916. The minimum age was 18 (19 for service abroad).

Follow up a line of research ...

Keep track of your railway ancestor by consulting documents deposited in the National Archives by one of the rail companies. The NA online catalogue will indicate if the specific records you're looking for are available. Content varies from one company to another but can include things like: name, age, job title, wage, and occasionally, a full service history. During WWI, and before conscription in 1916, company registers recorded the names of men who were prepared to join up.

Up close and personal

Photographs of servicemen can be dated reasonably accurately, and taking a close look at the uniforms will be an aid to researching their service records. Using a magnifying glass, try to identify the badges, insignia, and medals worn in the picture.

Local defence records

Contact the County Archives for details of any military collections they hold. These might concern local militia, volunteer, territorial, and home guard records.

Regimental museums and websites

A lot of regiments have their own museums, and many now have an online presence. The Imperial War Museum has an impressive collection of material on WWI and other conflicts involving Britain and the Commonwealth from 1914 to the present day. **www.iwm.org.uk**

News from the front ...

It can be profitable to search local newspapers covering the war years, especially if you know your ancestor was killed or badly wounded in action. Incidents involving local men were frequently reported on and can give details of the serviceman's regiment, his parents or wife, his address and his former place of employment.

War graves

The Commonwealth War Graves Commission has a database that lists the names of 1.7 million men and women of the Commonwealth forces who lost their lives in the two world wars. This 'Debt of Honour Register' is fully searchable online, and gives the cemetery or memorial where each individual is commemorated. **www.cwgc.org**

Quick tip

CIVILIAN WAR CASUALTIES
If one of your ancestors was a civilian and a casualty of the Second World War, my tip is to search the Dept of Honour Register as this also gives information about the 67,000 civilians who were killed as a result of enemy action.

DID YOU KNOW ...
During the 1914–1918 war, more than 700,000 women worked in the munitions industry.

WWI campaign medals

Campaign medals were awarded to men and women who saw active service overseas. The Medal Rolls Index, brought into being towards the end of the First World War, lists details of medal entitlement, rank and unit for all men and women who fought in the British Army or Royal Flying Corps. There's a free searchable database of the index at Documents Online, with a small charge to view the actual documents.

www.nationalarchives.gov.uk/documentsonline/medals.asp

A mention in Dispatches ...

The London Gazette published details of Honours and Awards during both World Wars; the entries have been indexed and can be searched free online. Your search phrase will bring up entries that have that exact wording so my tip is to try all variants – Frederick Smith, F. Smith, Smith F. and so on – though you'll have your work cut out just searching 'Smith'!

www.gazettes-online.co.uk

Women's Army Auxiliary Corps

Was your ancestor one of the 7,000 women who enrolled in the WAAC (1917-1918), later known as the Queen Mary's Army Auxiliary Corps (1918-1920)? There's lots of information to be had from the documents and enrolment forms.

www.nationalarchives.gov.uk/documentsonline/waac.asp

- Name, address, age, and names and addresses of next of kin.
- Location, grade, and promotions.
- ID certificate, references, casualty form, and uniform issued.

Quick tip

WAR DIARIES

War diaries were kept by officers during WWI and some of these — arranged by battalion — are now online, with the digital images downloadable for a small fee.
Put 'diary' into the search box to bring up the listing.
www.nationalarchives.gov.uk/documentsonline

Getting personnel!

If your forebear worked for the same firm over a long period, there could be a record of him in their personnel files. Businesses won't give out information about recent employees but might help with older records. And don't forget to ask County Archives and the local reference library — their ears might be worth bending when it comes to finding info about local firms.

Land Valuation

This involved a survey undertaken by the Inland Revenue around 1910; useful if your family were farmers or landowners. Those with less than 50 acres, and land worth less than £75 per acre were exempt, and a hefty fine faced any landowner who failed to declare! The Valuation Books are held in County Archives and give the names and addresses of owners and occupiers, a brief description of the property, and a map reference.

Throughly modern research!

School registers

When a school closes, which frequently happens with village schools especially, the admission registers are often deposited at County Archives. Although there's usually a closure period, these records can be worth tracking down as they give details of:

- Pupil's name and date of birth.
- Names and address of parents or guardians.
- The names and dates of birth of siblings.
- Date of admission to the school.
- Date and reason for leaving.

The best (or worst) days of their lives!

Your ancestor's good (or not so good) conduct at school might have been recorded in the school log book. These logs were kept by the head teacher and recorded the school's curriculum, special achievements by pupils, and prizes awarded. More everyday happenings were also noted, including illnesses and punishments for bad behaviour, or malingering and bunking off!

Back to school ...

School magazines often report on such things as which pupils were awarded certificates on speech day, who won the cup on sports day and who got the coveted leading role in the annual school production. Ask the school if such a magazine was ever produced – they might still have copies or someone could have deposited them in the County Archives.

The Aliens Registration Act 1914

The Act affected those aged 16 or over who moved to the UK from overseas. The compulsory registration documents give name and address, age, marital status, race, occupation, and employer. Surviving records can be found either at County Archives, or a local police archive.

We are sailing …

You might find the names of emigrating ancestors from 1906 to 1951 on the ships' passenger lists held at the National Archives.

- Annual lists of ships departing from Southampton, Bristol and Weymouth up until 1908.
- After 1908, monthly lists from other ports.
- From 1921, daily lists from every port.

Passage to Canada

Try the online database of ships' passengers at the Library and Archives Canada, if you're looking for family who arrived as immigrants in Canada between 1925 and 1935. Go through the 'Exploration and Settlement' link to reach the passengers' names database.
www.collectionscanada.ca

DID YOU KNOW …
Before 1882, a wife could only make a will with her husband's written consent.

In was the custom
in Victorian times
to cover all the
mirrors in the house
when someone died.

Thoroughly modern research!

Chapter summary:

- Records of clubs and societies are often deposited in local archives.
- The National Archives hold records of railway companies.
- Local businesses might have old personnel files.
- Newspapers frequently reported on local men injured in wartime.
- The Commonwealth War Graves Commission is a key resource.
- County Archives usually hold some military collections.
- Land Valuation Books give details of owners and occupiers.
- Many school records have been deposited with County Archives.
- School magazines can be very enlightening.
- The National Archives have ships' passenger lists for emigrants.

The great gift of family life is to be intimately acquainted with people you might never even introduce yourself to, had life not done it for you.

Kendall Hailey

Create your own family archive

chapter 10
Create your own family archive

Keeping notes

As filing systems go, a clear plastic pocket in a ring binder is a hard arrangement to beat. With each plastic sleeve labelled, the information can be found quickly, and data added to and rearranged whenever you discover something new.

It's a nice idea to compile a separate 'profile' for each of your ancestors, adding new information about them as and when you find it. Include dates and places along with all the relevant details of parents, birth or baptism, siblings, marriage, children, and death and burial. Then add in what you've unearthed about their home, their schooling, occupation or service history, and so on.

Always keep a record of the sources you've used: include the location, document title, index name, reference number, and date.

> **DID YOU KNOW ...**
> Small children are often noted as 'scholars' on census returns, even when they were under school age.

Preserving your documents

Dirt, light, heat, and moisture can all wreak havoc on your documents and photographs. Your family's history is worth preserving considering the time, effort and money you've put into the project, so think of the data you collected, not just as your research notes, but as a family legacy you'll be passing on to future generations.

When handling your documents, be sure that everything, from your hands to the surface you are working on, is free from dust and grease. Archivists, who are handling old records on a regular basis, wear special thin, white cotton gloves. So if you fancy kitting yourself out in a pair of these, they can be bought from suppliers of archival stationery.

Paper

Sunlight and fluorescent lighting can cause paper to yellow and ink to fade, while damp encourages spotting and mould. Aim to store your documents in a dry place that has a fairly constant temperature. Documents in archives are stored in temperature-controlled 'stacks', but most of us would find such temperatures a bit too low for comfort in our homes.

Paper contains natural acids which can affect the document itself by seeping out over a period of time. Newsprint is especially acidic, and is also more prone to discolouring. It's possible to buy acid-free folders to store records, and these will help prevent damage to individual documents as well as lowering the risk of papers contaminating each other. Clear plastic sleeves are best as they can be viewed without over-handling them.

Another good idea is to make copies of certain documents, and use these for reference, while storing the originals in a safe place.

Photos

Photographs are subject to all the same kind of environmental dangers as other documents – and then some.

Some photo albums might even damage your pictures over time, so keep your valuable prints in albums that are sold as 'archival quality', which means they're acid-free; or in special archive storage boxes, separating each photo with an acid-free sheet.

Copies of your old photographs should be processed by a dedicated photo lab, rather than by the sort that offers an express developing service, as this really is a specialist job.

Scanning prints, or making photocopies of them, is a cheaper option and although the strong light of the copying machine won't do your pictures any favours, they will only be exposed to this for a very short time.

Precious photos should never be laminated, as this process can damage the print.

DID YOU KNOW …
By the end of the 1800s, people were allowed books and newspapers, and children were allowed toys in the workhouse.

A bride adopting her husband's surname became the custom in the 15th century.

Useful addresses

Borthwick Institute of Historical Research,
University of York, Heslington,
York YO10 5DD
Tel 01904 321166

www.york.ac.uk/inst/bihr

College of Arms, Queen Victoria Street,
London EC4V 4BT
Tel 020 7248 2762

www.college-of-arms.gov.uk

The Family Records Centre,
1 Myddelton Street, Islington,
London EC1R 1UW
Tel 020 8392 5300

www.familyrecords.gov.uk

Federation of Family History Societies,
PO Box 2425,
Coventry, West Midlands CV5 6YX

www.ffhs.org.uk

General Register Office (England and Wales),
Certificate Services Section,
PO Box 2, Southport,
Merseyside PR9 2JD
Tel 0845 603 7788

www.gro.gov.uk

General Register Office (Ireland),
Government Offices, Convent Road, Roscommon, Eire
Tel 090 6632 900;

www.groireland.ie

General Register Office (Northern Ireland),
Oxford House,
49-55 Chichester Street, Belfast BT1 4HL
Tel 02890 252000

www.groni.gov.uk

General Register Office (Scotland),
New Register House,
3 West Register Street, Edinburgh EH1 3YT
Tel 0131 314 4433

www.gro-scotland.gov.uk

The National Archives,
Kew, Richmond, Surrey TW9 4DU
Tel 020 8876 3444

www.nationalarchives.gov.uk

National Archives of Ireland,
Bishop Street, Dublin 8, Eire
Tel 003531 4072300

www.nationalarchives.ie

National Archives of Scotland,
HM General Register House, Edinburgh EH1 3YY
Tel 0131 535 1314

www.nas.gov.uk

National Library of Wales,
Department of Manuscripts and Records,
Aberystwyth, Dyfed SY23 3BU, Wales
Tel 01970 632 800

www.llgc.org.uk

Principal Registry of the Family Division,
Probate Searchroom,
First Avenue House,
42-49 High Holborn, London WC1V 6NP
Tel 020 7947 7022

www.hmcourts-service.gov.uk/cms/wills.htm

Public Record Office of Northern Ireland,
66 Balmoral Avenue, Belfast BT9 6NY
Tel 028 9025 5905

www.proni.gov.uk

Religious Society of Friends Library,
Friends House,
Euston Road, London NW1 2BJ
Tel 020 7663 1135

www.quaker.org.uk

Society of Genealogists,
14 Charterhouse Buildings, Goswell Road,
London EC1M 7BA
Tel 020 7251 8799

www.sog.org.uk

Index

'The Greatest Tips in the World' books

Pet Recipe books

The Greatest Feline Feasts in the World by Joe Inglis
ISBN 978-1-905151-50-9

The Greatest Doggie Dinners in the World by Joe Inglis
ISBN 978-1-905151-51-6

'The Greatest in the World' DVDs

The Greatest in the World – Gardening Tips
presented by Steve Brookes

The Greatest in the World – Yoga Tips
presented by David Gellineau and David Robson

The Greatest in the World – Cat & Kitten Tips
presented by Joe Inglis

The Greatest in the World – Dog & Puppy Tips
presented by Joe Inglis

For more information about currently available
and forthcoming book and DVD titles please visit:

www.thegreatestintheworld.com

or write to:

The Greatest in the World Ltd
PO Box 3182
Stratford-upon-Avon
Warwickshire CV37 7XW
United Kingdom

Tel / Fax: +44(0)1789 299616
Email: info@thegreatestintheworld.com

The author

Maureen Vincent-Northam began researching local history in the 1980s. She's worked on a variety of projects with other writers, as well as in a local government department, and has contributed to newspapers, magazines and e-book workshops.

Her fascination with the past, and a bent for detective work, led to her involvement in genealogy. A family history researcher for seven years, she's helped scores of people worldwide to link up with their ancestors.

For more information visit her website at
www.maureen-vincent-northam.co.uk.